MW01292823

Spir   ____

Recipes

A Complete Cookbook of Spiralized
Dish Ideas!

Table of Contents

Introduction *4*

Wake your family up with tasty, spiralized breakfast dishes. Here are a few of the best… *6*

   1 – Spiralized Cheddar Broccoli Breakfast Muffins 7

   2 – Spiralized Breakfast Hash Browns 9

   3 – Sweet Potato Breakfast Shakshuka 11

   4 – Spiral Mexican Breakfast Burrito 14

   5 – Vegetarian Breakfast Quiche 17

There are SO many delicious recipes for lunch, dinner, side dishes and appetizers that make use of spiraled vegetables. Here are some of the best… *20*

   6 – Zoodles with Tomatoes & Chicken 21

   7 – Cranberry & Spiral Apple Salad 24

   8 – Spiral Potato Latkes 26

   9 – Spiral Papaya Thai Salad 29

10 – Zoodle & Cheese Medley *31*

   11 – Spiral Noodles with Ricotta & Spinach 33

   12 – Mexican Spiral Chips 36

   13 – Spicy Spiral Sweet Potatoes 38

   14 – Chicken Zoodle Alfredo 40

   15 – Cheesy Spiral Fries 43

   16 – Zoodle & Ricotta Lemon Chicken 45

17 – Squash & Beet Noodles 48

18 – Spiral Greek Salad.................................. 50

19 – Thai Spiral Zoodles 52

20 – Chicken 'n Zoodle Soup............................ 55

21 – Mexican Style Zoodles & Sauce................... 58

22 – Zoodle Shrimp Florentine 60

23 – Zoodle Puttanesca 63

24 – Zucchini Spiralized Pasta with Sauce 66

25 – Ginger & Sesame Spiralized Salad 68

Desserts made with a spiralizer? You bet! Here are some inspired choices... .... *71*

26 – Oat & Zucchini Cookies 72

27 – Spiral Apple Pie 75

28 – Zoodle Chocolate Doughnuts..................... 78

29 – Spiral Apple Crisp 81

30 – Plantain & Coconut Spiral-Rice Pudding.......... 84

Conclusion *86*

Introduction

Are you ready for some truly eye-opening recipes you can create with your spiralizer?

Regardless of the season, you can find fruits and vegetables that are easy to use for spiral recipes. And if summer is coming soon, you'll have heaps of wonderful produce that will be ready. Now you'll have some more interesting ways to include produce in recipes that are as tasty as can be.

Recipes with "zoodles" and other spiralized veggies are a lot healthier than dishes made with conventional noodles, since they have low fat and no bad carbohydrates to speak of.

Whether you want to start spiralizing slowly or jump right in, this cookbook will be very helpful for you. Mixtures of vegetable spirals make recipes seem familiar and more approachable for family members who prefer pasta or meats.

And you don't even NEED to buy a spiralizer to make these dishes! You can just use a vegetable peeler. It takes a bit longer, but the effect is largely the same. It might give you the push you've needed to buy a spiralizer, though, because they're fun to use!

Getting your family to eat more vegetables and fruits is a definite plus for everyone's good health. Once you know what a spiralizer can do, those trips to your local farmer's market may never be the same again. You'll be on the hunt for more spiralized, healthy meals.

Wake your family up with tasty, spiralized breakfast dishes. Here are a few of the best...

1 – Spiralized Cheddar Broccoli Breakfast Muffins

These muffins are like comfort food for breakfast, and there is healthy broccoli and cheese in each one. You'll even gain nutrients from using the broccoli florets and stems both.

Makes 12 Servings

Cooking + Prep Time: 25 minutes

Ingredients:

- 14 eggs, large
- 1 cup of broccoli florets, chopped
- 2 broccoli stems, large
- 1/4 cup of cheddar cheese shreds

Instructions:

1. Preheat oven to 400F.

2. Beat eggs in medium sized bowl.

3. Grease cups of muffin tin thoroughly. In each cup, add to 1/3 full with broccoli florets and noodles. Pour eggs over cups, filling to 3/4 full.

4. Sprinkle cups with cheese.

5. Bake at 400F for 15 to 20 minutes, till eggs have set completely. Remove pan from oven. Allow to cool for several minutes. Serve.

2 – Spiralized Breakfast Hash Browns

This great morning meal uses a simple and easy recipe and crisp potatoes to make it a tastier breakfast than traditional hash browns. Use a little corn starch if you want the exterior to be crispier.

Makes 4 Servings

Cooking + Prep Time: 45 minutes

Ingredients:

- 12 oz. of potatoes, Yukon Gold if available

- 1 & 1/2 tsp. of corn starch
- 1/2 tsp. of salt, kosher
- 2 tbsp. of oil, canola
- Non-stick spray

Instructions:

1. Run the potatoes through finest shredder blade in your spiralizer, forming long strands. Use a vegetable peeler if you don't have a spiralizer.

2. Place the potato strands flat on a few paper towel layers. Squeeze and blot out the excess moisture. Sprinkle with salt and corn starch. Toss lightly to coat.

3. Heat non-stick skillet on med. heat. Add the oil to your pan and swirl the pan to coat the bottom evenly.

4. Mound four spiral potato piles in the pan and flatten a bit. Cook for four or five minutes, till they are crisp and brown.

5. Coat the tops with non-stick spray and turn over the potato cakes. Cook for three or four minutes, till they are browned well. Serve promptly.

3 – Sweet Potato Breakfast Shakshuka

The spiral sweet potatoes really bulk up this breakfast dish, hailing originally from Israel. It offers more starches, nutrients and complex carbs than the original.

Makes 4 Servings

Cooking + Prep Time: 35 minutes

Ingredients:

- 1 tbsp. of oil, olive
- 1 sweet potato, large, spiralized and with noodles trimmed down a bit
- Salt, kosher

- Pepper, ground
- 2 & 1/4 cups of tomato puree
- 8 ounces of 1/4"-thick sliced round chorizo
- 2 minced cloves of garlic
- 1 tsp. of chili powder
- 1/2 tsp. of cumin, ground
- 4 eggs, large
- 1 sliced avocado
- 2 tbsp. of chopped cilantro, fresh

Instructions:

1. Preheat oven to 375F.

2. Heat oil in oven-safe skillet on med-high. After oil has begun to shimmer, add sweet potato noodles. Season as desired.

3. Cook sweet potato noodles till they wilt. Set aside. Add chorizo, tomato sauce, chili powder, cumin and garlic to oil. Stir often while cooking for 8-10 minutes, till flavors have melded. Taste and season as desired.

4. Add sweet potato noodles back into skillet. Toss in tomato mixture and coat. Form four indentations in tomato mixture. Crack an egg into each one.

5. Transfer skillet to oven. Bake for 10-14 minutes, till egg whites have set. Top with cilantro and avocado and serve promptly.

4 – Spiral Mexican Breakfast Burrito

This breakfast bowl in a burrito is made with eggs and spiralized sweet potatoes. It's a quick meal to make and it's also gluten free.

Makes 2 Servings

Cooking + Prep Time: 25 minutes

Ingredients:

- 1 sweet potato, large
- 1 tbsp. of oil, olive
- Salt, kosher
- Black pepper, ground
- 2 eggs, large
- 8 whites from large eggs
- 1/2 cup of salsa, + extra to top, as desired
- 1 diced avocado
- To garnish: cilantro, fresh

Instructions:

1. Spiralize potatoes with spiralizer.

2. Heat 2 tsp. oil in large sized pan on med. heat. Add potato noodles. Cook till they have just begun softening, about five to seven minutes. Season as desired.

3. Fill large-sized pot with several inches filtered water. Place on med-high heat till it begins simmering.

4. Crack eggs into simmering water. Keep them close to water surface. Cover pot. Turn heat off. Allow to set for four to five minutes. Eggs should be cooked but with soft centers.

5. Heat remaining 1 tsp. of oil in pan on med-high. Scramble egg whites till outsides are light golden brown in color.

6. Transfer cooked noodles to large sized bowl. Toss with 1/2 cup salsa till mixed well. Add scrambled egg whites in. Mix till dispersed well.

7. Divide noodles in two bowls. Top with cilantro and avocado + extra salsa, if you like. Serve.

5 – Vegetarian Breakfast Quiche

This quiche utilizes thin sliced potatoes for its crust. It's packed with super flavors like tomatoes, basil and zucchini noodles.

Makes 4 Servings

Cooking + Prep Time: 55 minutes

Ingredients:

- Non-stick spray
- 1 thinly sliced medium potato, russet

- 1/4 tsp. of garlic powder
- Salt, kosher
- Pepper, ground
- 6 eggs, large
- 1/3 cup of almond milk, plain, unsweetened
- Optional: 1/2 cup of cheese, mozzarella
- 4 leaves of basil
- 1 zucchini, small
- 1/2 cup of halved grape tomatoes

Instructions:

1. Preheat oven to 350F. Grease 9" pie plate using non-stick spray.

2. Arrange sliced potatoes and overlap so they cover sides and bottom of pie plate. Spray using non-stick spray. Season as desired.

3. Bake potato crust for 18-20 minutes, till tender. Allow to cool for five minutes.

4. Slice zucchini lengthways, half-way through. Do not pierce center. Slice into chips.

5. Whisk eggs, cheese, milk and basil together in medium sized bowl. Season as desired and add zoodles.

6. After potato crust is cooked tender, pour zucchini egg mixture over it. Pour tomatoes on top, evenly scattering them.

7. Bake crust and filling for 30-35 minutes, till eggs have set in center and puffed up elsewhere. Remove quiche from oven. Allow to cool for about five minutes. Slice and serve.

There are SO many delicious recipes for lunch, dinner, side dishes and appetizers that make use of spiraled vegetables. Here are some of the best...

6 – Zoodles with Tomatoes & Chicken

This handy recipe was inspired by the typical leftovers in our kitchen and pantry at the end of the week. Whether you use a spiralizer or a veggie peeler, it's a wonderful dish!

Makes 2 Servings

Cooking + Prep Time: 3/4 hour

Ingredients:

- 2 zucchini, large, with trimmed ends
- 2 tbsp. of oil, olive
- 12 halved cherry tomatoes
- 2 minced garlic cloves
- 1 tsp. of salt, kosher
- 1 tsp. of seasoning blend, Italian
- 1/2 tsp. of black pepper, fresh ground
- 1/2 cooked, chopped chicken breast
- 4 cups of spinach, baby
- 1/2 cup of peas, frozen
- 2 juiced lemons, fresh
- 1 zested lemon, fresh

Instructions:

1. Cut the zucchini into zoodles with spiralizer or vegetable peeler.

2. Heat 1 tbsp. of oil in large-sized skillet on med. heat. Add and stir tomatoes in. Cook till they begin browning, five to seven minutes. Add the garlic. Stir while cooking for 30-35 seconds.

3. Add zucchini and season as desired. Stir and combine well. Add peas, spinach, chicken, lemon zest and juice. Drizzle mixture with 1 tbsp. oil. Cover. Allow to simmer till heated fully through. Serve.

7 – Cranberry & Spiral Apple Salad

This simple 15 minute recipe is made with cranberries, apples, goat cheese and pecans. They are tossed together in a light dressing that really lets the flavors shine.

Makes 2-4 Servings

Cooking + Prep Time: 15 minutes

Ingredients:

- 1 apple, red
- 1 apple, Granny Smith
- 1/2 cup of poppy seed, citrus dressing, prepared

- 1/4 cup of cranberries, dried
- 1/4 cup of raisins, golden
- 1/4 cup of goat cheese crumbles
- 1/3 cup of chopped pecans

Instructions:

1. Spiralize apples. Toss them with dressing, then remainder of ingredients.

2. Serve promptly.

8 – Spiral Potato Latkes

This is a new approach to potato latkes. You'll shred the potatoes with a spiralizer, and the maple syrup and apples offer sweetness that allows these latkes to stand on their own.

Makes 4 Servings

Cooking + Prep Time: 25 minutes

Ingredients:

- 1 peeled apple, firm
- 1 peeled potato, russet
- 1 lightly beaten egg, large
- 3 tbsp. of flour, all-purpose
- 1 tsp. of syrup, maple
- 1/2 tsp. of salt, sea
- 1 pinch of nutmeg, ground
- 2 tbsp. of oil, vegetable, + extra if needed

Instructions:

1. Make deep vertical cuts on both sides of apple and potato.

2. Spiralize potato with small blade. Repeat spiralizing with the apple.

3. Spread the apple and potato shreds on paper towels and squeeze them to release excess moisture. Transfer them to bowl.

4. Mix the maple syrup, flour, egg, nutmeg and salt in the same bowl.

5. Heat the oil in skillet on med. heat. Add 2 tbsp. of apple mixture into skillet. Flatten a bit. Cook till the mixture is golden brown in color, which usually means about three to four minutes on each side. Drain on paper towels. Repeat with the rest of the mixture. Serve.

9 – Spiral Papaya Thai Salad

The spiralized papaya works wonderfully in this dish, also known as Som Tam. In Thailand, they eat papaya salad all the time. It's especially refreshing in the hot summer months.

Makes 4 Servings

Cooking + Prep Time: 1/2 hour

Ingredients:

- 1 peeled, halved, de-seeded papaya, green
- 6 chilis, red Thai

- 4 peeled garlic cloves
- 1 cup of 1"-cut green beans
- 2 juiced limes, fresh
- 4 tbsp. of fish sauce
- 4 chopped small tomatoes
- 4 tbsp. of peanuts, roasted

Instructions:

1. Spiralize papaya halves and set them aside.

2. Mash garlic with mortar and pestle. Add chili. Mash them together. Add green beans. Mash gently, only breaking beans open. Add peanuts. Mash again, lightly, to break up the peanuts.

3. Add lime juice and fish sauce to mixture. Use a spoon to toss and combine them.

4. Add tomatoes and papaya spirals to large sized bowl. Pour over garlic mixture. Toss and combine thoroughly. Mash papaya lightly, enough to soften it. Allow flavors to be absorbed, then serve.

10 – Zoodle & Cheese Medley

Broccoli stems belong in the spiralizer, not in the trash. They have lots of flavor and they're easy to serve when spiralized.

Makes 2 Servings

Cooking + Prep Time: 1/2 hour

Ingredients:

- 2 tbsp. of oil, olive, garlic-infused
- 1 spiral cut squash, Mexican

- 1 spiral cut squash, yellow
- 3 stems of spiral cut broccoli
- 1 pinch of garlic salt, +/- as desired
- Black pepper, ground, as desired
- 1 cup of cheddar cheese shreds
- 2 round-sliced chili peppers, Fresno type

Instructions:

1. Heat the oil in skillet on med. heat. Add both types of squash, stems of broccoli, garlic salt & pepper.

2. Stir constantly while cooking till veggies are becoming tender but are still firm when bitten.

3. Add and mix cheddar cheese shreds. Stir and cook till they melt, which typically takes between three and five minutes.

4. Transfer mixture to individual plates. Use Fresno chili peppers for garnishing. Serve.

11 – Spiral Noodles with Ricotta & Spinach

This dish holds butternut squash noodles with more than a hint of garlic, tossed with tomatoes and spinach. The ricotta and toasted pine nuts add their own tastes to this vegetarian-friendly meal.

Makes 2 Servings

Cooking + Prep Time: 25 minutes

Ingredients:

- 1 butternut squash, medium
- 2 tbsp. of pine nuts
- 1 tbsp. of oil, olive
- 1/2 tbsp. of garlic, minced
- 1/4 tsp. of pepper flakes, red
- 1/4 cup of sun-dried, thin-sliced tomatoes
- Zest from 1/2 fresh lemon
- Juice from 1/2 fresh lemon
- 2 cups of spinach, baby
- 1/2 cup of ricotta cheese
- 1/4 cup of parmesan cheese, grated
- Salt, kosher, as desired
- Pepper, ground, as desired

Instructions:

1. Slice ends of squash off and remove seeds. Peel portion remaining. Slice top off and you'll be left with two semi-flat ends. Spiralize them into squash noodles.

2. Heat large sized skillet on med. heat. Add the pine nuts. Toast them for two to three minutes till browned lightly. Set the pine nuts aside.

3. In the same large skillet, add oil, pepper flakes and garlic. Sauté for 25-30 seconds, till they are fragrant.

4. Add squash. Toss, coating in garlic and oil. Add a bit of water to skillet. Cover and cook for three to five minutes till noodles have softened a little.

5. Remove cover. Add tomatoes, baby spinach, lemon juice and lemon zest to skillet. Then toss and combine till spinach wilts. Season as desired.

6. Transfer the noodles to serving bowl and dollop ricotta cheese over the top. Use parmesan cheese and pine nuts to garnish. Serve.

12 – Mexican Spiral Chips

Store-bought potato chips are anything but healthy. Instead of buying a bag, make healthier zoodle chips yourself. The Mexican flavor is subtle and unique.

Makes 6 Servings

Cooking + Prep Time: 35 minutes

Ingredients:

- Non-stick spray, non-fat
- 2 unpeeled potatoes, russet
- 2 tsp. of seasoning mix, taco flavor, +/- as desired

- 2 tsp. of sriracha sauce, +/- as desired
- Salt, sea, as desired

Instructions:

1. Preheat the oven to 425F. Line cookie sheet with foil. Use non-stick spray on it.

2. Slice potatoes in long spirals with spiralizer or vegetable peeler. Cut those long spirals all into shorter strands.

3. Thread skewer through center of potato spirals. Push down gently so the spirals will fan out. Set the prepared skewers on cookie sheet from step 1. Spray using non-stick spray and sprinkle the taco seasoning blend on the top.

4. Roast in 425F oven till crisp and browned, which usually takes 15-18 minutes. Season using sea salt and sriracha, as desired. Serve.

13 – Spicy Spiral Sweet Potatoes

These spicy sweet potato spirals are a wonderful meatless appetizer or dinner. The crispy sweet potatoes are coated with chili powder and garlic, topped with guacamole.

Makes 4 Servings

Cooking + Prep Time: 1 & 1/4 hour

Ingredients:

- 3 spiralized sweet potatoes, medium
- Hot, filtered water + 1 tsp. of salt, kosher
- 2 tbsp. of oil, olive

- 1 tsp. of salt, kosher
- 1/2 tsp. of chili powder
- 1 tsp. of garlic powder
- 1/2 tsp. of cumin, ground
- Guacamole, prepared
- To garnish: lime wedges and diced green onions

Instructions:

1. Preheat oven to 475F.

2. Soak spiraled sweet potatoes in large bowl with salted hot water for 13-15 minutes. Remove them from water and pat them dry.

3. Return spirals to dry bowl. Toss with oil and seasonings till coated well.

4. Arrange spirals on foil-lined baking sheet. Bake for 45-60 minutes in 475F oven. Toss them every 20 minutes or so, till they have reached the crunchiness you desire.

5. Top with the guacamole. Garnish using lime wedges and green onions. Serve.

14 – Chicken Zoodle Alfredo

This is a great pseudo-pasta dish that is noodle free with zoodles, instead. The zoodles are garnished with sun-dried tomatoes and kissed with homemade garlicky Alfredo sauce.

Makes 6 Servings

Cooking + Prep Time: 1 & 1/4 hour

Ingredients:

- 1/3 cup of salt, kosher
- 2 cups of water, boiling
- 1 & 1/2 quarts of water, cold

- 4 strip-cut chicken breasts
- 6 zucchini
- 2 tbsp. of salt, kosher
- 1 tbsp. of oil, olive
- 9 tbsp. of butter, unsalted
- 6 garlic cloves
- 1 & 1/2 cups of cream, heavy
- 10 oz. of Parmesan cheese, grated
- 1 tsp. of black pepper, cracked
- 1/2 cup of grape tomatoes, halved, +/- as desired

Instructions:

1. Combine the salt in boiling water in large sized bowl and stir the water to dissolve the salt.

2. Add the cold water and the chicken strips. Place in the refrigerator for 1/2 to 1 hour. Drain the chicken and pat it dry.

3. Cut zucchini into 1/8" sliced with mandolin. Cut those slices into thinner strips; they will resemble fettuccini as far as thickness goes. Place them in bowl. Sprinkle with salt as desired. Allow to sit for 1/2 hour so they can soften.

4. Heat the oil in skillet on med. heat. Add the chicken and cook till all sides have browned and there is no pink inside. Transfer chicken to bowl.

5. Add the butter to same skillet, now on high heat. Crush the garlic into the skillet. Add the cream. Bring to boil. Reduce the heat down to med-low. Add Parmesan cheese.

6. Continuously whisk till cheese has melted fully and add pepper, as desired. Add the zucchini strips. Stir while cooking for one to two minutes.

7. Return the cooked chicken strips to skillet. Cook till they are warmed fully through. Toss and coat well. Season as desired and use tomatoes to garnish. Serve.

15 – Cheesy Spiral Fries

You can easily create these decadent but light spiralized fries for a snack or quick dinner. The cheese **Makes** the fries so tasty and delicious.

Makes 6 Servings

Cooking + Prep Time: 40 minutes

Ingredients:

For fries:

- 4 scrubbed potatoes, medium

- 1/4 tsp. of salt, kosher
- 1/2 tsp. of black pepper, cracked
- Non-stick spray, coconut oil

For nacho cheese:

- 5 oz. of cheddar cheese shreds, reduced-fat
- 1 tbsp. of corn starch
- 1 cup of milk, fat-free, evaporated
- Optional: 1 & 1/2 tsp. of hot sauce

Instructions:

1. To prepare the fries, preheat the oven to 375F.

2. Spiralize the potatoes into water bath. Then drain and pat them dry. Lay potato spirals onto a sheet pan. Spray with coconut oil spray. Season as desired. Bake for 12-20 minutes, till tender and golden.

3. To prepare the nacho cheese, toss corn starch and cheese shreds together in med. sized sauce pan. Add the milk. Cook on low and stir continuously till thickened and melted. Add hot sauce, if desired. Top the fries with 1/4 cup of cheese sauce and serve.

16 – Zoodle & Ricotta Lemon Chicken

This lemon chicken and zoodle recipe is flavorful yet light. It's a wonderful way to utilize your abundant summer harvest.

Makes 4 Servings

Cooking + Prep Time: 3/4 hour + 3-8 hours refrigeration time

Ingredients:

- 4 strip-cut halved chicken breasts, boneless, skinless
- 4 minced garlic cloves
- 1 zested lemon
- 1 tbsp. of chives, chopped
- 1 tsp. of thyme, fresh
- 1 tsp. of oregano, fresh
- 1/2 tsp. of salt, kosher
- 1/4 tsp. of pepper, ground
- 1/4 cup of oil, olive + extra for the pan
- 4 spiralized zucchinis
- 1 pinch of pepper flakes, red
- Salt, kosher, as desired
- Pepper, ground, as desired
- 1 & 1/2 cups of cheese, ricotta
- 4 chopped basil leaves, fresh
- 1 lemon, juiced
- 2 diced tomatoes, fresh
- 2 fresh tomatoes, diced

Instructions:

1. Place the chicken strips, garlic, chives, oregano, thyme, lemon zest, 1/4 cup of oil and salt & pepper as desired in zipper top plastic bag. Toss and coat the chicken. Place in refrigerator for at least three hours, or overnight.

2. Heat large sized skillet on med. heat. Stir while cooking chicken with the marinade until the meat isn't pink in center anymore. Internal temperature should be 165F or higher. Remove the chicken from the pan and set it aside. Keep it warm.

3. Drizzle 1 tsp. of oil in same skillet on med-high. Add zucchini and pepper flakes. Cook till zucchini has warmed. Season as desired.

4. Stir basil and ricotta cheese into the zucchini. Cook till heated fully through.

5. Return the chicken to the pan with the zucchini mixture and combine by stirring. Remove the pan from heat. Squeeze the lemon juice over the entire dish. Use diced tomatoes to garnish. Serve.

17 – Squash & Beet Noodles

If you like roasted beets, you will LOVE spiralized beets. A spiralizer or veggie peeler turns squash and beets into twirling, tasty noodles in a delightful sauce.

Makes 4 Servings

Cooking + Prep Time: 20 minutes

Ingredients:

- 1 peeled beet, medium
- 1 peeled golden beet, medium

- 1 peeled squash, butternut
- 1 tbsp. + 2 tsp. oil, olive
- 1/2 cup of parsley, Italian
- 3/8 tsp. of salt, kosher
- 1/2 tsp. of black pepper, cracked
- 1 lemon, zest only
- 1 oz. of crumbled feta cheese

Instructions:

1. Spiralize the beets and neck of butternut squash.

2. Combine veggies with a bit of water in glass bowl. Place in microwave oven and cook for a minute or so, till tender. Drain squash noodles and beets on paper towels.

3. In food processor or blender, combine the parsley, 1 tbsp. of oil, lemon zest, kosher salt and cracked pepper. Blend till you have a smooth texture.

4. Toss spiralized vegetables gently in the pesto sauce. Sprinkle using feta cheese and serve.

18 – Spiral Greek Salad

Zoodles are so popular these days, and unique recipes show you new ways they can be prepared. A love for Greek salads, plus a love for zoodles, equals a great alternative to traditional pasta.

Makes 4 Servings

Cooking + Prep Time: 1/2 hour

Ingredients:

- 2 zucchinis
- 1/4 chopped cucumber, English
- 10 halved cherry tomatoes
- 10 pitted, halved kalamata olives

- 1/4 cup of red onion, sliced thinly
- 2 oz. of crumbled feta cheese, reduced fat
- 2 tbsp. of oil, olive
- 2 tbsp. of lemon juice, fresh
- 1 tsp. of oregano, dried
- Salt, kosher, as desired
- Black pepper, ground, as desired

Instructions:

1. Spiralize the zucchinis into noodle-like strands with spiralizer or vegetable peeler. Place these zoodles in large sized bowl. Top them with the tomatoes, cucumber, red onion, olives & feta cheese.

2. Whisk the lemon juice, oil and oregano in bowl and season as desired. Whisk till the dressing has become smooth. Pour it over the zoodle mixture. Toss and coat well.

3. Marinate the salad in your refrigerator for 10-15 minutes. Serve.

19 – Thai Spiral Zoodles

The nut butter, coconut milk and fresh curry paste in this recipe make an easy but complex-tasting satay sauce. You can use it like a dip or in a stir-fry, or drizzle it on zoodles, as I have here.

Makes 4 Servings

Cooking + Prep Time: 1/2 hour

Ingredients:

- 2 & 1/2 tbsp. of sesame oil, toasted
- 2 spiralized sweet potatoes, medium
- 1 cup of bell pepper, red, sliced thinly
- 3/4 tsp. of salt, kosher
- 1/2 cup of water, filtered
- 3 cups of spinach, baby
- 8 oz. of 1/2" cubed tofu, extra firm
- 1/2 cup of coconut milk, light, canned
- 3 tbsp. of butter, almond
- 2 tbsp. of curry paste, fresh
- 1/4 cup of chopped cashews, unsalted
- 4 wedges of fresh lime

Instructions:

1. Heat 1 & 1/2 tbsp. of oil in large, heavy skillet on med-high. Add the bell pepper, sweet potato noodles and 1/2 tsp. of salt. Sauté for five minutes.

2. Add 1/4 cup of filtered water and cover the skillet. Cook for three minutes. Remove cover and cook for two more minutes. Add spinach and stir till it wilts. Place the potato mixture in bowl.

3. Add the last 1 tbsp. of oil to the pan. Add the tofu. Stir occasionally while sautéing for four minutes.

4. Combine last 1/4 cup of filtered water, last 1/4 tsp. of kosher salt, along with almond butter, coconut milk, and the curry paste in medium bowl.

5. Add 1/2 cup of sauce to the potato mixture and toss. Divide the potato mixture into four bowls. Evenly top them with tofu, the rest of the sauce and the cashews. Garnish with one lime wedge per bowl and serve.

20 – Chicken 'n Zoodle Soup

When the cold months of winter approach, this remake of classic chicken noodle soup is a winner. It's comforting and warm and doesn't have the calories of "real" noodles.

Makes 6 Servings

Cooking + Prep Time: 50 minutes

Ingredients:

- 2 tbsp. of oil, olive
- 1 cup of onions, diced
- 1 cup of celery, diced
- 3 minced garlic cloves
- 5 x 14 & 1/4 oz. cans of chicken broth, low-sodium
- 1 cup of carrots, sliced
- 3/4 lb. of bite-size cubed chicken breast, cooked
- 1/2 tsp. of basil, dried
- 1/2 tsp. of oregano, dried
- Optional: 1 pinch of thyme, dried
- Salt, kosher, as desired
- Pepper, ground, as desired
- 3 zucchinis, cut in "zoodles" with spiralizer or veggie peeler

Instructions:

1. Heat oil in large sized pot on med-high. Sauté the garlic, onion and celery in the heated oil till barely tender, for five minutes or so.

2. Pour the broth in the pot. Add the chicken, carrots, thyme, oregano, basil, kosher salt & ground pepper.

3. Bring broth to boil, then reduce the heat down to med-low. Simmer the mixture till vegetables have become tender. This usually takes 15-20 minutes.

4. Divide the zoodles among six individual bowls and ladle the broth & mixture over them. Serve.

21 – Mexican Style Zoodles & Sauce

Elote is a popular Mexican street food, and this dish includes the same grilled corn with chili powder, mayo, queso fresco and a zesty lime squeeze. It is served as a fresh zoodle salad.

Makes 4 Servings

Cooking + Prep Time: 10-15 minutes

Ingredients:

- 3/4 cup of corn kernels, fresh
- 2 tbsp. of chopped cilantro, fresh
- 1 & 1/2 tbsp. of oil, olive

- 1 tbsp. of lime juice, fresh
- 1/4 tsp. of salt, kosher
- 1 trimmed, spiralized zucchini, large
- 2 tbsp. of sour cream, light
- 2 tsp. of water, filtered
- 2 tbsp. of crumbled cheese, queso fresco
- 1/8 tsp. of red pepper, ground

Instructions:

1. Place the first six ingredients in large sized bowl and toss them.

2. Combine 2 tsp. of filtered water with sour cream and drizzle this over the zucchini-corn-etc. mixture.

3. Top the mixture with crumbled cheese & red ground pepper and serve.

22 – Zoodle Shrimp Florentine

This is a great recipe for trying out your spiralizer for the first time. You can sprinkle the dish with a bit of Old Bay seasoning or Parmesan cheese.

Makes 4 Servings

Cooking + Prep Time: 1/2 hour

Ingredients:

- 1 tbsp. of butter, unsalted
- 1 tbsp. of oil, olive

- 2 spiralized zucchinis
- 1/2 minced large onion, yellow
- 1 tbsp. of garlic, chopped
- 1/2 tsp. of salt, kosher
- 2 tbsp. of butter, unsalted
- 1 lb. of peeled, de-veined shrimp, large
- 1 tsp. of garlic, minced
- 1 x 6-oz. bag of spinach, baby
- 1 tbsp. of lemon juice, fresh
- 1 tsp. of pepper flakes, red
- 1/2 tsp. of salt, kosher
- 1/2 tsp. of black pepper, ground

Instructions:

1. Heat oil and 1 tbsp. of unsalted butter together in large sized skillet on med. heat. Stir while cooking the zoodles, chopped garlic, onion & 1/2 tsp. of kosher salt till onion becomes translucent and zoodles become tender. This usually takes five minutes or so. Transfer this zoodle mixture into a large bowl.

2. Heat 2 tbsp. of unsalted butter in same skillet. Stir while cooking minced garlic and shrimp till the shrimp are barely pink, or three to four minutes.

3. Add lemon juice, pepper flakes, spinach, 1/2 tsp. of salt and ground pepper. Stir and cook till spinach has begun wilting, or three to four minutes or so. Add the zoodle mixture. Stir and cook till mixture is heated fully through. Serve.

23 – Zoodle Puttanesca

You'll be replacing heavy pasta with hearty sweet potato spirals in this Paleo-friendly meal. It's named after the savory Italian dish.

Makes 6 Servings

Cooking + Prep Time: 20 minutes

Ingredients:

- 1/4 cup of oil, olive
- 6 minced cloves of garlic

- 4 fillets, anchovy
- 1 & 1/2 tsp. of oregano, dried
- 3/4 tsp. of red pepper, crushed
- 2 cups of chicken stock, unsalted
- 6 cups of sweet potatoes, spiralized
- 3 pints of halved cherry tomatoes, multi-colored
- 2 tbsp. of tomato paste, unsalted
- 1/4 cup of chopped basil, fresh
- 1/4 cup of chopped parsley, fresh
- 24 pitted, chopped kalamata olives
- 3 tbsp. of capers
- 1/8 tsp. of salt, kosher

Instructions:

1. Heat sauté pan with high sides on med. heat. Add the oil to the pan and swirl, coating it. Add the red pepper, oregano, anchovies and garlic. Cook for two minutes while constantly stirring, so you will break up the anchovies.

2. Add the stock. Bring to boil. Add and stir tomato paste, spiral sweet potatoes and tomatoes.

3. Cook for two to three minutes, till sweet potato spirals are softened slightly. Remove the pan from heat and add the remaining ingredients. Combine by tossing and serve.

24 – Zucchini Spiralized Pasta with Sauce

Do you love pasta but want a healthier option? Zoodles are as close to the real deal as you can find. This is a quick and versatile recipe, too.

Makes 1 Serving

Cooking + Prep Time: 15-20 minutes

Ingredients:

- 2 peeled zucchinis
- 1 tbsp. of oil, olive
- 1/4 cup of water, filtered

- Kosher salt & ground pepper, as desired
- Prepared sauce, your favorite

Instructions:

1. Use vegetable peeler or spiralizer to make zoodles from the zucchinis. The strips should resemble spaghetti in shape.

2. Heat the oil in skillet on med. heat. Stir while cooking zoodles in heated oil for a minute. Add the water. Cook till the zoodles are soft, about five to seven minutes. Season as desired. Serve.

25 – Ginger & Sesame Spiralized Salad

Summer picnics can boast the best ice cream and vegetables, as well as hot dogs and hamburgers. This simple ginger and sesame cucumber salad is a winner.

Makes 4-6 Servings

Cooking + Prep Time: 30 minutes

Ingredients:

For the salad

- 2 julienned carrots, medium
- 2 English cucumbers, large
- 1 & 1/2 cups of frozen, defrosted edamame, shelled
- 1 tbsp. of sesame seeds, black, white or mixture, toasted

For dressing

- 1 & 1/2 tbsp. of water, warm or hot
- 2 & 1/2 tbsp. of miso, white
- 2 tbsp. of vinegar, rice
- 1 tbsp. plus 1 tsp. of peeled ginger, grated
- 1 tbsp. of maple syrup or honey
- 1 tbsp. plus 1 tsp. of oil, sesame
- 2 tsp. of lemon juice, fresh
- 1/2 tsp. of soy sauce or tamari sauce

Instructions:

1. Use a spiralizer to make "noodles" from cucumber. Toss them with carrots and edamame.

2. Whisk water and miso together in small bowl till completely smooth in texture. Add remainder of dressing ingredients. Combine by whisking. Taste, then adjust as desired.

3. Toss veggies with the dressing. You can use half the dressing or all, whatever you prefer. Sprinkle top with sesame seeds. Serve.

Desserts made with a spiralizer? You bet! Here are some inspired choices...

26 – Oat & Zucchini Cookies

These delicious cookies are gooey and gluten-free. The apple butter is a healthy sweetener and the oats do not dry the cookies out at all.

Makes 24 Servings

Cooking + Prep Time: 15 minutes

Ingredients:

For the dry mixture

- 1 cup of flour, gluten-free
- 1 tsp. of baking soda
- 1/2 tsp. of salt, kosher
- 3/4 tsp. of cinnamon, ground

For the wet mixture

- 1/4 cup of apple butter
- 1 egg, large
- 3/4 cup of sugar, brown
- 1 tsp. of vanilla extract, pure
- 1 cup of zucchini spirals
- 2 cups of rolled oats, gluten-free
- 1/2 cup of white chocolate chips, mini

Instructions:

1. Preheat oven to 350F. Line cookie sheet with baking paper.

2. Whisk the flour, salt, baking soda and ground cinnamon together in medium bowl. Set the bowl aside.

3. Add brown sugar and apple butter to large sized bowl. Mix till brown sugar has melted into apple butter and mixture is smooth. Whisk in vanilla and egg. Add zucchini spirals. Combine by whisking.

4. Stir flour mixture into apple butter mixture till barely combined. Add and fold in chocolate chips and oats.

5. Scoop dough with 1 tbsp. scoop on prepared, lined cookie sheet. Leave three inches between the cookies.

6. Bake for 10-12 minutes, till edges are a bit golden brown in color. Allow cookies to rest on cookie sheet for three to five minutes. Transfer to wire rack for full cooling. Serve.

27 – Spiral Apple Pie

This pie offers the same taste as classic apple pie. You can even toss in some nuts or dried fruit to give it more of an autumn taste.

Makes 8 Servings

Cooking + Prep Time: 1 & 1/4 hour

Ingredients:

- 2 pie crusts, refrigerated

- 2 & 1/2 lbs. of firm apples, like Granny Smith or Honeycrisp
- 1 tbsp. of lemon juice, fresh squeezed
- 1 cup of sugar, granulated
- 1/4 cup of corn starch
- 1/2 tsp. of cinnamon, ground
- 1/2 tsp. of ginger, ground
- 1 tsp. of vanilla extract, pure
- 2 tbsp. of butter, unsalted, cubed in eight cubes
- Optional: cream and turbinado sugar

Instructions:

1. Preheat oven to 375F.

2. Unroll first prepared pie crust. Place in 9" pie plate. Cut and fold any excess dough under edges, creating a scalloped edge of the crust. Prick holes across bottom of crust. Freeze crust in pan for 15 minutes or longer as you're preparing filling.

3. Rinse apples, but do not peel. Spiralize them. Discard the cores and stems. Toss apple spirals in lemon juice.

4. Whisk sugar, cinnamon, ginger and corn starch together in medium bowl. Mix gently into apple spirals. If they break, that's ok.

5. Pour filling into crust. Place cubes of butter evenly across surface of filling.

6. Unroll second pie crust. Use it to top pie. Cut slits for escaping steam.

7. Brush top crust area but not edges with cream. Sprinkle using sugar as desired.

8. Bake pie for 40-45 minutes, till filling is bubbly and crust is a golden brown color. Cool fully, then slice and serve.

28 – Zoodle Chocolate Doughnuts

These decadent doughnuts are Paleo-friendly and gluten-free. The recipe uses tapioca and coconut flours instead of more processed flours. It even includes vegan chocolate chips.

Makes 6 Servings

Cooking + Prep Time: 35 minutes

Ingredients:

- 1 zucchini, medium

- 1/2 cup of flour, coconut
- 1/4 cup of flour, tapioca
- 3/4 tsp. of baking soda
- 1/4 tsp. of salt, kosher
- 2 tsp. of cinnamon, ground
- 1/2 tsp. of nutmeg, ground
- 1 & 1/2 tbsp. of cacao powder
- 3 eggs, large
- 3 tbsp. of syrup, maple
- 2 tsp. of vanilla extract, pure
- 2 tsp. of milk, almond
- 1 tbsp. of oil, coconut
- 1 mashed banana, ripe
- 2 tbsp. of unsweetened coconut, shredded

For chocolate

- 1/4 cup of chocolate chips, vegan

Instructions:

1. Preheat oven to 350F. Grease doughnut tin with non-stick spray and set tin aside.

2. Spiralize zucchini into zoodles. Pour both flours, salt, baking soda, nutmeg, cinnamon and the cacao into medium bowl.

3. In separate bowl, mix syrup, eggs, almond milk, vanilla extract, banana and coconut oil together.

4. Add dry ingredients to wet mixture. Add zucchini. Stir till you have a smooth batter.

5. Pour batter into doughnut tins. Bake for 25-30 minutes, till inserted toothpick comes back clean.

6. Carefully pop doughnuts out.

7. Place small sized sauce pan on med-high heat. Add chocolate chips. Allow them to heat and stir them frequently, till they have melted fully.

8. Place doughnuts on baking paper. Drizzle chocolate on top. Use coconut flakes for dusting. They can be served right away, or you can let them sit for 15 to 20 minutes so the chocolate hardens.

29 – Spiral Apple Crisp

A spiralizer will be easier to use than peeling and slicing the apples for this recipe. The noodle-y texture is an enjoyable version of traditional apple crisp desserts.

Makes 12 Servings

Cooking + Prep Time: 1 hour & 20 minutes

Ingredients:

For the filling

- 6 apples, Granny Smith

- 3 tbsp. of sugar, light brown, packed
- 2 tbsp. of lemon juice, fresh
- 1 tbsp. of corn starch
- 1/2 tsp. of cinnamon, ground
- 1/4 tsp. of salt, kosher

For the topping

- 1 & 1/2 cups of oats
- 1/2 cup of almond meal
- 4 tbsp. of melted butter, unsalted
- 1/3 cup of sugar, light brown, packed
- 1 tsp. of cinnamon, ground
- 1/2 tsp. of salt, kosher

Instructions:

1. Preheat oven to 350F. Coat 13" x 9" baking dish using non-stick spray.

2. Cut apples into long strands with spiralizer or vegetable peeler. Toss them with lemon juice, 3 tbsp. of brown sugar, corn starch, 1/2 tsp. of cinnamon & 1/4 tsp. of salt in large sized bowl. Transfer to prepared pan.

3. Combine almond meal, oats, 1/3 cup of brown sugar, 1 tsp. of cinnamon & 1/2 tsp. of salt in medium sized bowl. Add and stir butter. Crumble mixture over fruit. Bake till apples become soft, the filling bubbles around edges and topping is a golden brown color. This typically takes 50-55 minutes. Allow to cool five minutes. Serve.

30 – Plantain & Coconut Spiral-Rice Pudding

This pudding is sweetened with plantains, with a subtle taste, not one that overwhelms you. Cinnamon and raisins with coconut offer additional texture and sweetness.

Makes 1 Serving

Cooking + Prep Time: 10-15 minutes

Ingredients:

- 1 & 1/3 cup of milk, vanilla almond
- 1 plantain, peeled, medium-ripe
- 1/8 tsp. of cinnamon, ground
- 1/4 cup of raisins
- 1 to 2 tsp. of flaked coconut

Instructions:

1. Place plantain noodles in food processor. Pulse till they are in bits, which look like rice. Place them in medium sized sauce pan. Add 1 cup of almond vanilla milk.

2. Bring contents of pan to boil. Once it is boiling, then lower heat to simmer and simmer for 8-10 minutes. Rice should reduce by five minutes. At that time, add in remaining 1/3 cup milk. Allow the mixture to reduce further. Stir it occasionally till it is creamy.

3. Once that is done, remove pan from the heat. Add coconut flakes, raisins and cinnamon. Stir till cinnamon has dissolved into pudding. Serve.

Conclusion

This spiralizing cookbook has shown you...

How to use different ingredients to create unique tastes in spiral dishes that are healthier and just as tasty as their pasta counterparts.

How can you include spiralized ingredients in your home recipes?

You can...

- Make spiral-enhanced breakfast treats, both sweet and savory. They are just as tasty as they sound.
- Learn to cook with zucchinis, which are widely used in spiral recipes. Many people think zucchinis are the ONLY vegetable used in a spiralizer, but they aren't.
- Enjoy making the delectable spaghetti-type spirals that are as easy to mix with sauces and other veggies as well. Faux pasta is a mainstay in spiral recipes, and there are SO many ways to make them great.

- Make dishes using all kinds of veggies, which are utilized well in spiralized cooking.
- Make various types of spiral-enhanced desserts like apple pie and chocolate doughnuts with zoodles that will tempt your family's sweet tooth.

Have fun experimenting! Enjoy the results!

Made in the USA
Las Vegas, NV
21 February 2022

44317222R00048